Healtl

Air Fryer

Grill Cookbook

50 Best Healthy Grill Recipes For Your Air Fryer Device

Susan Harris

TABLE OF CONTENTS

INTRODUCTION

The Air Fryer Grill is a unique and innovative kitchen appliance that allows for healthy, oil-free cooking! With a capacity of up to 6lbs, it can be used to make everything from cuts of beef for sandwiches to large batches of fries.

Benefits include:

- No Oils Needed!

With this machine, you can cook using your favorite foods, without the use of oil

- Features a Non-Stick Tray

This feature allows you to place marinated meats or vegetables directly on the grill, and be able to wipe it clean!

- 360 Degree Control

The control panel gives you 360 degrees of heat control from high to low, and every option in between.

- Adjustable Temperature

With an adjustable temperature, you can cook your food at just the right temperature for delicious results each time.

- Cooks Food Faster than Traditional Methods!

Cooking at lower temperatures and with the air circulation eliminates the risk of burning foods, and allows you to cook meats, vegetables and other foods while they are still fresher.

- Multiple Features

This product also includes a digital timer to help you monitor your cooking, and two removable racks that allow you to cook multiple items at once.

- Easy Cleaning!

The non-stick tray makes cleanup easy! You can use soap and water to clean it, or wipe it clean with a damp cloth!

- Value for Price

Priced at only $99 this product is an excellent value for the quality features it offers.

- Let's Food Breathe Under Low Pressure!

The air fryer allows foods to cook in their natural juices and with the circulation of hot air, it helps foods cook faster and more evenly.

The Air Fryer Grill is a unique and innovative kitchen appliance that allows for healthy, oil-free cooking! With a capacity of up to 6lbs, it can be used to make everything from cuts of beef for sandwiches to large batches of fries. The Air Fryer Grill is a must-have for anyone that wants to cook foods without using oil.

Pros:

5,400 BTU Dimension: 13 x 8 x 6 inches Features: The Air Fryer Grill is a non-stick grill that features a frame made from foldable black metal. It offers an adjustable thermostat and two racks with handles to hold your food as it cooks. It also includes an on/off switch, a digital timer, and an indicator light. The Air Fryer Grill is a must-have for anyone that wants to cook foods without using oil. It comes with non-stick racks for easier cleanup. Cons: The Air Fryer Grill does not have any cons so far.

Taste: Unlike other air fryers, the Air Fryer Grill allows you to cook at lower temperatures, which leaves your food fresher and tastier because it allows the natural juices to remain in your foods as they cook. Airtight Cooking System: Most air fryers require open flame to cook food, but the Air Fryer Grill has an airtight system that cooks food with minimal mess. Adjustable Temperature: The Air Fryer Grill has the option for low and high heat settings. It allows you to cook at lower temperatures for food that is less fatty, and serve your fries at a higher temperature for a crunchier experience. Safety Features: The Air Fryer Grill features a non-stick tray that makes cleaning easy, and also helps your food to cook in their natural juices. Several Colors Available: The Air Fryer Grill comes in several colors including white with black metal frame, red with black metal frame, or a white color with red stem.

BREAKFAST

1. Chinese Style Cod

Preparation Time: 5 minutes

Cooking Time: 10 minutes

Servings: 2

Ingredients:

- 2 medium cod fillets; boneless
- 1 tbsp. light soy sauce
- 1/2 tsp. ginger; grated
- 1 tsp. peanuts; crushed
- 2 tsp. garlic powder

Directions:

1. Put fish fillets in a heat proof dish that fits your air fryer, add garlic powder, soy sauce and ginger; toss well, put in your air fryer and cook at 350 °F, for 10 minutes.
2. Divide fish on plates, sprinkle peanuts on top and serve.

Nutrition: Calories: 254; Fat: 10; Fiber: 11; Carbs: 14; Protein: 23

2. Almond Flour Coco-Milk Battered Chicken

Preparation Time: 5 minutes

Cooking Time: 30 minutes

Servings: 4

Ingredients:

- ¼ cup coconut milk
- ½ cup almond flour
- 1 ½ tablespoons old bay Cajun seasoning
- 1 egg, beaten
- 4 small chicken thighs
- Salt and pepper to taste

Directions:

1. Preheat the air fryer for 5 minutes
2. Mix the egg and coconut milk in a bowl.
3. Soak the chicken thighs in the beaten egg mixture.
4. In a mixing bowl, combine the almond flour, Cajun seasoning, salt and pepper.
5. Dredge the chicken thighs in the almond flour mixture.
6. Place in the air fryer basket.
7. Cook for 30 minutes at 3500F.

Nutrition: Calories 590 Carbs3.2g Protein 32.5 g
Fat 38.6g

3. Bacon 'n Egg-Substitute Bake

Preparation Time: 5 minutes

Cooking Time: 30 minutes

Servings: 4

Ingredients:

- 1 (6 ounce) package Canadian bacon, quartered
- 1/2 cup 2% milk
- 1/4 teaspoon ground mustard
- 1/4 teaspoon salt
- 2 cups shredded Cheddar-Monterey Jack cheese blend
- 3/4 cup and 2 tablespoons egg substitute (such as Egg Beaters® Southwestern Style)
- 4 frozen hash brown patties

Directions:

1. Lightly grease baking pan of air fryer with cooking spray.
2. Evenly spread hash brown patties on bottom of pan. Top evenly with bacon and then followed by cheese.
3. In a bowl, whisk well mustard, salt, milk, and egg substitute. Pour over bacon mixture.
4. Cover air fryer baking pan with foil.

5. Preheat air fryer to 330oF.
6. Cook for another 20 minutes, remove foil and continue cooking for another 15 minutes or until eggs are set.
7. Serve and enjoy.

Nutrition: Calories 459 Carbs 21.0g Protein 29.4g Fat 28.5g

4. Baked Rice, Black Bean and Cheese

Preparation Time: 5 minutes

Cooking Time: 1 hour

Servings: 4

Ingredients:

- 1 cooked skinless boneless chicken breast halves, chopped
- 1 cup shredded Swiss cheese
- 1/2 (15 ounce) can black beans, Dry out
- 1/2 (4 ounce) can diced green chili peppers, Dry out
- 1/2 cup vegetable broth
- 1/2 medium zucchini, thinly sliced
- 1/4 cup sliced mushrooms
- 1/4 teaspoon cumin
- 1-1/2 teaspoons olive oil
- 2 tablespoons and 2 teaspoons diced onion
- 3 tablespoons brown rice
- 3 tablespoons shredded carrots
- Ground cayenne pepper to taste
- Salt to taste

Directions:

1. Lightly grease baking pan of air fryer with cooking spray. Add rice and broth. Cover pan with foil cook for 10 minutes at 390oF. Lower heat to 300oF and fluff rice. Cook for another 10 minutes Let it stand for 10 minutes and transfer to a bowl and set aside.
2. Add oil to same baking pan. Stir in onion and cook for 5 minutes at 330oF.
3. Stir in mushrooms, chicken, and zucchini. Mix well and cook for 5 minutes
4. Stir in cayenne pepper, salt, and cumin. Mix well and cook for another 2 minutes
5. Stir in ½ of the Swiss cheese, carrots, chilies, beans, and rice. Toss well to mix. Evenly spread in pan. Top with remaining cheese.
6. Cover pan with foil.
7. Cook for 15 minutes at 390oF and then remove foil and cook for another 5 to 10 minutes or until tops are lightly browned.
8. Serve and enjoy.

Nutrition: Calories 337 Carbs 11.5g Protein 25.3g Fat 21.0g

5. BBQ Chicken Recipe from Greece

Preparation Time: 5 minutes

Cooking Time: 24minutes

Servings: 2

Ingredients:

- 1 (8 ounce) container fat-free plain yogurt
- 2 tablespoons fresh lemon juice
- 2 teaspoons dried oregano
- 1-pound skinless, boneless chicken breast halves - cut into 1-inch pieces
- 1 large red onion, cut into wedges
- 1/2 teaspoon lemon zest
- 1/2 teaspoon salt
- 1 large green bell pepper, cut into 1 1/2-inch pieces
- 1/3 cup crumbled feta cheese with basil and sun-dried tomatoes
- 1/4 teaspoon ground black pepper
- 1/4 teaspoon crushed dried rosemary

Directions:

1. In a shallow dish, mix well rosemary, pepper, salt, oregano, lemon juice, lemon zest, feta

cheese, and yogurt. Add chicken and toss well to coat. Marinate in the ref for 3 hours.

2. Thread bell pepper, onion, and chicken pieces in skewers. Place on skewer rack.

3. For 12 minutes, cook it on 360oF. Turnover skewershalfway through cooking time. If needed, cook in batches.

4. Serve and enjoy.

Nutrition: Calories 242 Carbs 12.3g Protein 31.0g Fat 7.5g

6. BBQ Pineapple 'n Teriyaki Glazed Chicken

Preparation Time: 5 minutes

Cooking Time: 20 minutes

Servings: 2

Ingredients:

- ¼ cup pineapple juice
- ¼ teaspoon pepper
- ½ cup brown sugar
- ½ cup soy sauce
- ½ teaspoon salt
- 1 green bell pepper, cut into 1-inch cubes
- 1 red bell pepper, cut into 1-inch cubes
- 1 red onion, cut into 1-inch cubes
- 1 Tablespoon cornstarch
- 1 Tablespoon water
- 1 yellow red bell pepper, cut into 1-inch cubes
- 2 boneless skinless chicken breasts cut into 1-inch cubes
- 2 cups fresh pineapple cut into 1-inch cubes
- 2 garlic cloves, minced
- Green onions, for garnish

Directions:

1. In a saucepan, bring to a boil salt, pepper, garlic, pineapple juice, soy sauce, and brown sugar. In a small bowl whisk well, cornstarch and water. Slowly stir in to mixture in pan while whisking constantly. Simmer until thickened, around 3 minutes. Save ¼ cup of the sauce for basting and set aside.
2. In shallow dish, mix well chicken and remaining thickened sauce. Toss well to coat. Marinate in the ref for a half hour.
3. Thread bell pepper, onion, pineapple, and chicken pieces in skewers. Place on skewer rack in air fryer.
4. For 10 minutes, cook on 360oF. Turnover skewers halfway through cooking time. and baste with sauce. If needed, cook in batches.
5. Serve and enjoy with a sprinkle of green onions.

Nutrition: Calories 391 Carbs 58.7g Protein 31.2g Fat 3.4g

7. BBQ Turkey Meatballs with Cranberry Sauce

Preparation Time: 5 minutes

Cooking Time: 20 minutes

Servings: 4

Ingredients:

- 1 ½ tablespoons of water
- 2 teaspoons cider vinegar
- 1 tsp. salt and more to taste
- 1-pound ground turkey
- 1 1/2 tablespoons barbecue sauce
- 1/3 cup cranberry sauce
- 1/4-pound ground bacon

Directions:

1. In a bowl, mix well with hands the turkey, ground bacon and a tsp. of salt. Evenly form into 16 equal sized balls.
2. In a small saucepan boil cranberry sauce, barbecue sauce, water, cider vinegar, and a dash or two of salt. Mix well and simmer for 3 minutes
3. Thread meatballs in skewers and baste with cranberry sauce. Place on skewer rack in air fryer.

4. For 15 minutes, cook it on 360oF. Every after 5 minutes of cooking time, turnover skewers and baste with sauce. If needed, cook in batches.
5. Serve and enjoy.

Nutrition: Calories 217 Carbs 11.5g Protein 28.0g Fat 10.9g

8. Spicy Herb Chicken Wings

Preparation Time: 15 minutes

Cooking Time: 15 minutes

Servings: 6

Ingredients:

- 4 lbs. chicken wings
- ½ tablespoon ginger
- 2 tablespoons vinegar
- 1 fresh lime juice
- 1 tablespoon olive oil
- 2 tablespoons soy sauce
- 6 garlic cloves, minced
- 1 habanero, chopped
- ¼ teaspoon cinnamon
- ½ teaspoon sea salt

Directions:

1. Preheat your air fryer to 390°Fahrenheit.
2. Add ingredients to a large bowl and combine well.
3. Place chicken wings into the marinade mix and store in the fridge for 2 hours.
4. Add chicken wings to the air fryer and cook for 15-minutes. Serve hot!

Nutrition: Calories 673 Fat 29g Carbs 9g Protein 39g

9. Sweet & Sour Chicken Skewer

Preparation Time: 5 minutes

Cooking Time: 18 minutes

Servings: 4

Ingredients:

- 1 lb. of chicken tenders
- ¼ teaspoon of pepper
- 4 garlic cloves, minced
- 1 ½ tablespoons soy sauce
- 2 tablespoons pineapple juice
- 1 tablespoon sesame oil
- ½ teaspoon ginger, minced

Directions:

1. Preheat your air fryer to 390°Fahrenheit.
2. Combine ingredients in a bowl, except for the chicken.
3. Skewer the chicken tenders' then place in a bowl and marinate for 2-hours.
4. Add tenders to the air fryer and cook for 18-minutes. Serve hot!

Nutrition: Calories: 217 Fat 3g Carbs: 15.3g Protein 21.3g

10. Greek Chicken

Preparation Time: 10 minutes

Cooking Time: 15 minutes

Servings: 4

Ingredients:

- 2 tablespoons olive oil
- Juice from 1 lemon
- 1 teaspoon oregano, dried
- 3 garlic cloves, minced
- 1-pound chicken thighs
- Salt and black pepper to the taste
- ½ pound asparagus, trimmed
- 1 zucchini, roughly chopped
- 1 lemon sliced

Directions:

1. In a heat proof dish that fits your air fryer, mix chicken pieces with oil, lemon juice, oregano, garlic, salt, pepper, asparagus, zucchini and lemon slices, toss, introduce in preheated air fryer and cook at 380 degrees F for 15 minutes Divide everything on plates and serve. Enjoy!

Nutrition: Calories 300 Fat 8 Carbs 20 Protein 18

11. Duck Breasts with Red Wine and Orange Sauce

Preparation Time: 10 minutes

Cooking Time: 35 minutes

Servings: 4

Ingredients:

- ½ cup honey
- 2 cups orange juice
- 4 cups red wine
- 2 tablespoons sherry vinegar
- 2 cups chicken stock
- 2 teaspoons pumpkin pie spice
- 2 tablespoons butter
- 2 duck breasts, skin on and halved
- 2 tablespoons olive oil
- salt and black pepper to the taste

Directions:

2. Heat up a pan with the orange juice over medium heat, add honey, stir well and cook for 10 minutes Add wine, vinegar, stock, pie spice and butter, stir well, cook for 10 minutes more and take off heat.

3. Season duck breasts with salt and pepper, rub with olive oil, place in preheated air fryer at 370 degrees F and cook for 7 minutes on each side.
4. Divide duck breasts on plates, Drizzle with wine and orange juice all over and serve right away. Enjoy!

Nutrition: Calories 300 Fat 8 Carbs 24 Protein 11

12. Grilled Salmon

Preparation Time: 5 minutes

Cooking Time: 10 minutes

Servings: 3

Ingredients:

- 2 Salmon Fillets
- 1/2 Tsp Lemon Pepper
- 1/2 Tsp Garlic Powder
- Salt and Pepper
- 1/3 Cup Soy Sauce
- 1/3 Cup Sugar
- 1 Tbsp. Olive Oil

Directions:

1. Season salmon fillets with lemon pepper, garlic powder and salt. In a shallow bowl, add a third cup of water and combine the olive oil, soy sauce and sugar. Place salmon the bowl and immerse in the sauce. Cover with cling film and allow to marinate in the refrigerator for at least an hour
2. Preheat the Innsky air fryer at 350 degrees.

3. Place salmon into the Air fryer and cook for 10 minutes or more until the fish is tender. Serve with lemon wedges

Nutrition: Calories: 185 kcal Protein: 5.16 g Fat: 11.74 g Carbohydrates: 16.06 g

13. Crispy Paprika Fish Fillets

Preparation Time: 5 minutes

Cooking Time: 15 minutes

Servings: 4

Ingredients:

- 1/2 cup seasoned breadcrumbs
- 1 tablespoon balsamic vinegar
- 1/2 teaspoon seasoned salt
- 1 teaspoon paprika
- 1/2 teaspoon ground black pepper
- 1 teaspoon celery seed
- 2 fish fillets, halved
- 1 egg, beaten

Directions:

1. Add the breadcrumbs, vinegar, salt, paprika, ground black pepper, and celery seeds to your food processor. Process for about 30 seconds.
2. Coat the fish fillets with the beaten egg; then, coat them with the breadcrumbs mixture.
3. Cook at 350 degrees F for about 15 minutes.

Nutrition: Calories: 208 kcal Protein: 15.19 g Fat: 9.44 g Carbohydrates: 11.61 g

14. Bacon Wrapped Shrimp

Preparation Time: 5 minutes

Cooking Time: 5 minutes

Servings: 4

Ingredients:

- 1¼ pound tiger shrimp, peeled and deveined
- 1-pound bacon

Directions:

1. Wrap each shrimp with a slice of bacon.
2. Refrigerate for about 20 minutes. Preheat the Innsky air fryer to 390 degrees F.
3. Arrange the shrimp in the Air fryer basket. Cook for about 5-7 minutes.

Nutrition: Calories: 514 kcal Protein: 42.66 g Fat: 36.92 g Carbohydrates: 7.17 g

15. Bacon-Wrapped Scallops

Preparation Time: 5 minutes

Cooking Time: 10 minutes

Servings: 4

Ingredients:

- 16 sea scallops
- 8 slices bacon, cut in half
- 8 toothpicks
- Salt
- Freshly ground black pepper

Directions:

1. Using a paper towel, pat dry the scallops.
2. Wrap each scallop with a half slice of bacon. Secure the bacon with a toothpick.
3. Place the scallops into the air fryer in a single layer. (You may need to cook your scallops in more than one batch.)
4. Spray the scallops with olive oil, and season them with salt and pepper.
5. Set the temperature of your Innsky AF to 370°F. Set the timer and fry for 5 minutes.
6. Flip the scallops.

7. Reset your timer and cook the scallops for 5 minutes more.

8. Using tongs, remove the scallops from the air fryer basket. Plate, serve, and enjoy!

Nutrition: Calories: 311 Fat: 17g Saturated fat: 5g Carbohydrate: 3g Fiber: 0g Sugar: 0g Protein: 34g Sodium: 1110mg

16.Air Fryer Salmon

Preparation Time: 5 minutes

Cooking Time: 10 minutes

Servings: 2

Ingredients:

- ½ tsp. salt
- ½ tsp. garlic powder
- ½ tsp. smoked paprika
- Salmon

Directions:

1. Mix spices together and sprinkle onto salmon. Place seasoned salmon into the Air fryer.
2. Close crisping lid. Set temperature to 400°F, and set time to 10 minutes.

Nutrition: Calories: 185 Fat: 11g; Protein: 21g Sugar: 0g

17. Lemon Pepper, Butterand Cajun Cod

Preparation Time: 5 minutes

Cooking Time: 12 minutes

Servings: 2

Ingredients:

- 2 (8-ounce) cod fillets, cut to fit into the air fryer basket
- 1 tablespoon Cajun seasoning
- ½ teaspoon lemon pepper
- 1 teaspoon salt
- ½ teaspoon freshly ground black pepper
- 2 tablespoons unsalted butter, melted
- 1 lemon, cut into 4 wedges

Directions:

1. Spray the Innsky air fryer basket with olive oil. Place the fillets on a plate. In a small mixing bowl, combine the Cajun seasoning, lemon pepper, salt, and pepper.
2. Rub the seasoning mix onto the fish.
3. Place the cod into the greased air fryer basket. Brush the top of each fillet with melted butter.
4. Set the temperature of your Innsky AF to 360°F. Set the timer and bake for 6 minutes.

After 6 minutes, open up your air fryer drawer and flip the fish. Brush the top of each fillet with more melted butter.

5. Reset the timer and bake for 6 minutes more. Squeeze fresh lemon juice over the fillets.

Nutrition: Calories: 377 kcal Protein: 23.49 g Fat: 26.1g Carbohydrates: 11.8 g

18. Steamed Salmon & Sauce

Preparation Time: 5 minutes

Cooking Time: 10 minutes

Servings: 2

Ingredients:

- 1 cup Water
- 2 x 6 oz. Fresh Salmon
- 2 Tsp Vegetable Oil
- A Pinch of Salt for Each Fish
- ½ cup Plain Greek Yogurt
- ½ cup Sour Cream
- 2 tbsp. Finely Chopped Dill (Keep a bit for garnishing)
- A Pinch of Salt to Taste

Directions:

1. Pour the water into the bottom of the fryer and start heating to 285° F.
2. Drizzle oil over the fish and spread it. Salt the fish to taste.
3. Now pop it into the fryer for 10 min.
4. In the meantime, mix the yogurt, cream, dill and a bit of salt to make the sauce. When the

fish is done, serve with the sauce and garnish with sprigs of dill.

Nutrition: Calories: 223 kcal Protein: 12.12 g Fat: 16.62 g Carbohydrates: 7.72 g

19. Salmon Patties

Preparation Time: 5 minutes

Cooking Time: 10 minutes

Servings: 4

Ingredients:

- 1 (14.75-ounce) can wild salmon, drained
- 1 large egg
- ¼ cup diced onion
- ½ cup bread crumbs
- 1 teaspoon dried dill
- ½ teaspoon freshly ground black pepper
- 1 teaspoon salt
- 1 teaspoon Old Bay seasoning

Directions:

1. Spray the Innsky air fryer basket with olive oil. Put the salmon in a medium bowl and remove any bones or skin. Add the egg, onion, bread crumbs, dill, pepper, salt, and Old Bay seasoning and mix well. Form the salmon mixture into 4 equal patties. Place the patties in the greased air fryer basket.
2. Set the temperature of your Innsky AF to 370°F. Set the timer and grill for 5 minutes.

Flip the patties. Reset the timer and grill the patties for 5 minutes more. Plate, serve, and enjoy.

Nutrition: Calories: 239; Fat: 9g Saturated fat: 2g Carbohydrate: 11g Fiber: 1g Sugar: 1g Protein: 27g Iron: 2mg Sodium: 901mg

20.   Pesto Bruschetta

Preparation Time: 10 minutes

Cooking Time: 10 minutes

Servings: 4

Ingredients:

- 8 slices French bread, ½ inch thick
- 2 tablespoons softened butter
- 1 cup shredded mozzarella cheese
- ½ cup basil pesto
- 1 cup chopped grape tomatoes
- 2 green onions, thinly sliced

Directions:

1. Spread the bread with the butter and place butter-side up in the air fryer basket. Bake it for 3 to 5 minutes or until the bread is light golden brown.
2. Remove the bread from the basket and top each piece with some of the cheese. Return to the basket in batches and bake until the cheese melts, about 1 to 3 minutes. Meanwhile,

combine the pesto, tomatoes, and green onions in a small bowl.

3. When the cheese has melted, remove the bread from the air fryer and place on a serving plate. Top each slice with some of the pesto mixture and serve.

Nutrition: Calories 462 Fat 25g Carbs 41g Protein 19g

21. Fried Tortellini with Spicy Dipping Sauce

Preparation Time: 10 minutes

Cooking Time: 20 minutes

Servings: 4

Ingredients:

- ¾ cup mayonnaise
- 2 tablespoons mustard
- 1 egg
- ½ cup flour
- ½ teaspoon dried oregano
- 1½ cups bread crumbs
- 2 tablespoons olive oil
- 2 cups frozen cheese tortellini

Directions:

1. In a small bowl, combine the mayonnaise and mustard and mix well. Set aside.In a shallow bowl, beat the egg. In a separate bowl, combine the flour and oregano. In another bowl, combine the bread crumbs and olive oil, and mix well.

2. Drop the tortellini, a few at a time, into the egg, then into the flour, then into the egg again, and

then into the bread crumbs to coat. Put into the air fryer basket, cooking in batches.

3. Air-fry for about 10 minutes, shaking halfway through the cooking time, or until the tortellini are crisp and golden brown on the outside. Serve with the mayonnaise.

Nutrition: Calories 698; Fat 31g Carbs 88g Protein 18g

22. Shrimp Toast

Preparation Time: 12 minutes

Cooking Time: 15 minutes

Servings: 4

Ingredients:

- 3 slices firm white bread
- ⅔ cup finely chopped peeled and deveined raw shrimp
- 1 egg white
- 2 cloves garlic, minced
- 2 tablespoons cornstarch
- ¼ teaspoon ground ginger
- Pinch salt
- Freshly ground black pepper
- 2 tablespoons olive oil

Directions:

1. Cut the crusts from the bread using a sharp knife; crumble the crusts to make bread crumbs. Set aside. In a small bowl, combine the shrimp, egg white, garlic, cornstarch, ginger, salt, and pepper, and mix well.

2. Spread the shrimp mixture evenly on the bread to the edges. With a sharp knife, cut each slice into 4 strips.

3. Mix the bread crumbs with the olive oil and pat onto the shrimp mixture. Place the shrimp toasts in the air fryer basket in a single layer; you may need to cook in batches.

4. Air-frying it for 3 to 6 minutes, until crisp and golden brown

Nutrition: Calories 121; Fat 6g Carbs 7g Protein 9g

23. Bacon Tater Tots

Preparation Time: 5 minutes

Cooking Time: 17 minutes

Servings: 4

Ingredients:

- 24 frozen tater tots
- 6 slices precooked bacon
- 2 tablespoons maple syrup
- 1 cup shredded Cheddar cheese

Directions:

1. Put the tater tots in the air fryer basket. Air-fry for 10 minutes, shaking the basket halfway through the cooking time
2. Meanwhile, cut the bacon into 1-inch pieces and shred the cheese.
3. Remove the tater tots from the air fryer basket and put into a 6-by-6-by-2-inch pan. Top with the bacon and Drizzle with the maple syrup. Air-fry for 5 minutes or until the tots and bacon are crisp.
4. Top with the cheese and air-fry for 2 minutes or until the cheese is melted.

Nutrition: Calories 374 Fat 22g Carbs 34g Protein
13g

24. Hash Brown Burchett

Preparation Time: 10 minutes

Cooking Time: 10 minutes

Servings: 4

Ingredients:

- 4 frozen hash brown patties
- 1 tablespoon olive oil
- ⅓ cup chopped cherry tomatoes
- 3 tablespoons diced fresh mozzarella
- 2 tablespoons grated Parmesan cheese
- 1 tablespoon balsamic vinegar
- 1 tablespoon minced fresh basil

Directions:

1. Place the hash brown patties in the air fryer in a single layer. Air-fry for 6 to 8 minutes or until the potatoes are crisp, hot, and golden brown.
2. Meanwhile, combine the olive oil, tomatoes, mozzarella, Parmesan, vinegar, and basil in a small bowl. When the potatoes are done, carefully remove from the basket and arrange on a serving plate. Top with the tomato mixture and serve.

Nutrition: Calories 123 Fat 6g Carbs 14g Protein 5g

25. Waffle Fry Poutine

Preparation Time: 10 minutes

Cooking Time: 20 minutes

Servings: 4

Ingredients:

- 2 cups frozen waffle cut fries
- 2 teaspoons olive oil
- 1 red bell pepper, chopped
- 2 green onions, sliced
- 1 cup shredded Swiss cheese
- ½ cup bottled chicken gravy

Directions:

1. Toss the waffle fries with olive oil and place in the air fryer basket. Air-fry for 10 to 12 minutes or until the fries are crisp and light golden brown, shaking the basket halfway through the cooking time.
2. Transfer the fries to a 6-by-6-by-2-inch pan and top with the pepper, green onions, and cheese. Air-fry for 3 minutes until the vegetables are crisp and tender.
3. Remove the pan from the air fryer and Drizzle with the gravy over the fries. Air-fry for 2

minutes or until the gravy is hot. Serve immediately.

Nutrition: Calories 347; Fat 19g Carbs 33g Protein 12g

26. Crispy Beef Cubes

Preparation Time: 10 minutes

Cooking Time: 20 minutes

Servings: 4

Ingredients:

- 1-pound sirloin tip, cut into 1-inch cubes
- 1 cup cheese pasta sauce (from a 16-ounce jar)
- 1½ cups soft bread crumbs
- 2 tablespoons olive oil
- ½ teaspoon dried marjoram

Directions:

1. In a medium bowl, toss the beef with the pasta sauce to coat.
2. In a shallow bowl, combine the bread crumbs, oil, and marjoram, and mix well. Drop the beef cubes, one at a time, into the bread crumb mixture to coat thoroughly.
3. Cook the beef in two batches for 6 to 8 minutes, shaking the basket once during cooking time, until the beef is at least 145°F and the outside is crisp and brown. Serve with toothpicks or little forks.

Nutrition: Calories 554 Fat 22g Carbs 43g Protein 44g

27. Buffalo Chicken Bites

Preparation Time: 10 minutes

Cooking Time: 18 minutes

Servings: 4

Ingredients:

- ⅔ cup sour cream
- ¼ cup creamy blue cheese salad dressing
- ¼ cup crumbled blue cheese
- 1 celery stalk, finely chopped
- 1-pound chicken tenders, cut into thirds crosswise
- 3 tablespoons Buffalo chicken wing sauce
- 1 cup panko bread crumbs
- 2 tablespoons olive oil

Directions:

1. In a small bowl, combine the sour cream, salad dressing, blue cheese, and celery, and set aside.
2. In a medium bowl, combine the chicken pieces and Buffalo wing sauce and stir to coat. Let sit while you get the bread crumbs ready.
3. Combine the bread crumbs and olive oil on a plate and mix.

4. Coat the chicken pieces in the bread crumb mixture, patting each piece so the crumbs adhere.

5. Air-fry in batches for 7 to 9 minutes, shaking the basket once, until the chicken is cooked to 165°F and is golden brown. Serve with the blue cheese sauce on the side.

Nutrition: Calories 467; Fat 23g Carbs 22g Protein 43g

28. Grilled Avocado Caprese Crostini

Preparation Time: 10 minutes

Cooking Time: 20 minutes

Servings: 2

Ingredients:

- 1 avocado thinly sliced
- 9 ounces ripened cherry tomatoes
- Ounces fresh bocconcini in water
- 2 tsp balsamic glaze
- 8 pieces Italian baguette
- ½ cup basil leaves

Directions:

1. Preheat your oven to 375 degrees Fahrenheit
2. Arrange your baking sheet properly before spraying them on top with olive oil.
3. Bake your item of choice until they are well done or golden brown. Rub your crostini with the cut side of garlic while they are still warm and you can season them with pepper and salt.
4. Divide the basil leaves on each side of bread and top up with tomato halves, avocado slices and bocconcini. Season it with pepper and salt.

5. Broil it for 4 minutes and when the cheese starts to melt through remove and Drizzle with balsamic glaze before serving.

Nutrition: Calories 278 Fat 10g Carbs 37g Proteins 10g

29. Caprese Stuffed Garlic Butter Portobellos

Preparation Time: 5 minutes

Cooking Time: 10 minutes

Servings: 6

Ingredients:

- For Garlic butter
- 2 tsp of butter
- 2 cloves garlic 1 tsp parsley finely chopped
- For the mushrooms
- 6 large Portobello mushrooms, washed and dried well with paper towel
- 6 mozzarella cheese balls thinly sliced
- 1 cup grape tomatoes thinly sliced
- Fresh basil for garnishing
- For balsamic glaze
- 2 tsp brown sugar
- ¼ cup balsamic vinegar

Directions:

1. Preheat the oven to broil setting on high heat. Arrange the oven shelf and place it in the right direction. Combine the garlic butter ingredients in a small pan and melt until the garlic begins to be fragrant. Brush the bottoms of the

mushroom and place them on the buttered part of the baking tray.

2. Flip and brush the remaining garlic over each cap. Fill each mushroom with tomatoes and mozzarella slices and grill until the cheese has melted. Drizzle with the balsamic glaze and sprinkle some salt to taste. If you are making the balsamic glaze from scratch, combine the sugar and vinegar in a small pan and reduce the heat to low. Allow it to simmer for 6 minutes or until the mixture has thickened well.

Nutrition: Calories 101 Fat 5g, Carbs 12g, Proteins 2g

30. Tomato Soup

Preparation Time: 10 minutes

Cooking Time: 7 minutes

Servings: 4

Ingredients:

- 2 tablespoons of homemade tomato sauce
- 2 teaspoons of dried basil, crushed
- 4 cups of low-sodium vegetable broth
- 1 tablespoon of balsamic vinegar
- 3 pounds of fresh tomatoes, chopped
- 1 tablespoon of olive oil
- 2 teaspoons of dried parsley, crushed
- 2 tablespoons of sugar
- 1 medium onion, chopped
- Freshly ground black pepper, to taste
- ¼ cup of fresh basil, chopped
- 1 garlic clove, minced

Directions:

1. Set the Instant Vortex on Air fryer to 365 degrees F for 5 minutes

2. Put the tomatoes, garlic, onion, and fresh basil in the cooking tray.
3. Insert the cooking tray in the Vortex when it displays "Add Food". Remove from the Vortex when cooking time is complete.
4. Put the olive oil in a wok and add the tomatoes mixture, tomato sauce, dried herbs, broth, and black pepper.
5. Secure the lid of the wok and cook for about 12 minutes on medium heat.
6. Fold in the sugar and vinegar.
7. Pour into the immersion blender and puree the soup to serve hot.

Nutrition: Calories 146 Fat 4.5g Carbs 23.5g Protein 5.4g

31. Roasted Tomatoes

Preparation Time: 5 minutes

Cooking Time: 8 minutes

Servings: 4

Ingredients:

- 1 tablespoon of herbed butter
- 4 large tomatoes
- 1 cup of mozzarella cheese, shredded

Directions:

1. Set the Instant Vortex on Roast to 365 degrees F for 10 minutes Scoop out the internal filling of the tomatoes and stuff with the cheese.
2. Place the stuffed tomatoes on the cooking tray and top with the herbed butter. Insert the cooking tray in the Vortex when it displays "Add Food". Remove from the Vortex when cooking time is complete. Serve warm.

Nutrition: Calories 75 Fat 3.2 Carbs 7.5g Protein 5g

32. Corn Kernels

Preparation Time: 5 minutes

Cooking Time: 5 minutes

Servings: 4

Ingredients:

- 2 tablespoons of butter
- Salt and black pepper, to taste
- 1½ cups of corn kernels
- 1 tablespoons of lemon juice

Directions:

1. Set the Instant Vortex on Air fryer to 375 degrees F for 6 minutes Season the corn kernels with red pepper, salt and black pepper.
2. Squeeze the lemon juice on the corn kernels and top with butter. Place the corn kernels on the cooking tray.
3. Insert the cooking tray in the Vortex when it displays "Add Food".
4. Remove from the Vortex when cooking time is complete. Serve warm.

Nutrition: Calories 18 Fat 6.7g Carbs 32.2g Protein 5.6g

33.   Bacon Potato Cheesy Soup

Preparation Time: 5 minutes

Cooking Time: 20 minutes

Servings: 4

Ingredients:

- 1 cup of cheddar cheese, shredded
- 1 cup of frozen corn
- 3 tablespoons of butter
- ¼ teaspoon of red paprika flakes
- 8 large potatoes, peeled and cubed
- 1 teaspoon of salt
- 2 cups of half and half cream
- 1 teaspoon of black pepper
- 2 tablespoons of dried parsley
- 3 oz. of cream cheese, cubed
- 6 slices bacon, crumbled
- ½ cup of onions, chopped
- 3 cups of chicken broth

Directions:

1. Set the Instant Vortex on Air fryer to 375 degrees F for 5 minutes Put the potatoes, corn, and bacon in the cooking tray.

2. Insert the cooking tray in the Vortex when it displays "Add Food". Remove from the Vortex when cooking time is complete.
3. Put the butter in a wok and add the onions. Sauté for about 3 minutes and fold in the potato's mixture with rest of the ingredients.
4. Secure the lid of the wok and cook for about 12 minutes on medium heat.
5. Dish out the potatoes, mash them well and return to the pot.
6. Stir the soup well and serve hot.

Nutrition: Calories 669 Protein 20 g Carbs 88g Fat 28g

34. Bacon and Cauliflower Soup

Preparation Time: 10 minutes

Cooking Time: 20 minutes

Servings: 4

Ingredients:

- 2 tablespoons of butter
- 4 cups of chicken stock
- 1 large onion, chopped
- 4 potatoes, chopped
- 3 cups of cauliflower florets
- ½ cup of heavy cream
- 1 tablespoon of salt
- 1 tablespoon of black pepper
- 12 slices of bacon, crisp fried

Directions:

1. Set the Instant Vortex on Air fryer to 375 degrees F for 5 minutes Put the bacon, potatoes, and cauliflower in the cooking tray. Insert the cooking tray in the Vortex when it displays "Add Food". Remove from the Vortex when cooking time is complete. Put the butter in a wok and add the onions.

2. Sauté it for about 3 minutes and then stirs in the bacon mixture and the chicken stock. Secure the lid of the wok and cook for about 10 minutes on medium heat. Pour this mixture into an immersion blender and puree it. Ladle out in a bowl to serve.

Nutrition: Calories 344 Protein 8.3g Carbs 44.1g Fat 16.7g

35. Simple & Delicious Spiced Apples

Preparation Time: 10 minutes

Cooking Time: 10 minutes

Servings: 4

Ingredients:

- 4 apples, sliced
- 1 tsp apple pie spice
- 2 tbsp. sugar
- 2 tbsp. ghee, melted

Directions:

1. Add apple slices into the mixing bowl.
2. Add remaining ingredients on top of apple slices and toss until well coated.
3. Transfer apple slices on instant vortex air fryer oven pan and air fry at 350 F for 10 minutes.
4. Top with ice cream and serve.

Nutrition: Calories – 196 Protein– 0.6 g Fat – 6.8 g Carbs – 37.1 g.

36. Tangy Mango Slices

Preparation Time: 10 minutes

Cooking Time: 12 hours

Servings: 6

Ingredients:

- 4 mangoes, peel and cut into ¼-inch slices
- 1/4 cup fresh lemon juice
- 1 tbsp. honey

Directions:

1. In a big bowl, combine together honey and lemon juice and set aside.
2. Add mango slices in lemon-honey mixture and coat well.
3. Arrange mango slices on instant vortex air fryer rack and dehydrate at 135 F for 12 hours.

Nutrition: Calories – 147 Protein– 1.9 g Fat – 0.9 g Carbs – 36.7 g.

37. Dried Raspberries

Preparation Time: 10 minutes

Cooking Time: 15 hours

Servings: 4

Ingredients:

- 4 cups raspberries, wash and dry
- 1/4 cup fresh lemon juice

Directions:

1. Add raspberries and lemon juice in a bowl and toss well.
2. Arrange raspberries on instant vortex air fryer oven tray and dehydrate at 135 F for 12-15 hours.
3. Store in an air-tight container.

Nutrition: Calories – 68 Protein– 1.6 g Fat – 0.9 g Carbs – 15 g.

38. Crispy Dumplings

Preparation Time: 10 minutes

Cooking Time: 10 minutes

Servings: 8

Ingredients:

- .5 lb. Ground pork
- 1 tbsp. Olive oil
- .5 tsp each Black pepper and salt
- Half of 1 pkg. Dumpling wrappers

Directions:

1. Set the Air Fryer temperature setting at 390° Fahrenheit.
2. Mix the fixings together.
3. Prepare each dumpling using two teaspoons of the pork mixture.
4. Seal the edges with a portion of water to make the triangle form.
5. Lightly spritz the Air Fryer basket using a cooking oil spray as needed. Add the dumplings to air-fry for eight minutes.
6. Serve when they're ready.

Nutrition: Calories: 110 kcal Protein: 8.14 g Fat: 8.34 g Carbohydrates: 0.27 g

39. Pork Joint

Preparation Time: 10 minutes

Cooking Time: 20 minutes

Servings: 10

Ingredients:

- 3 cups Cooked shredded pork tenderloin or chicken
- cups Fat-free shredded mozzarella
- 10 small Flour tortillas
- Lime juice

Directions:

1. Set the Air Fryer at 380° Fahrenheit.
2. Sprinkle the juice over the pork.
3. Microwave five of the tortillas at a time (putting a damp paper towel over them for 10 seconds). Add three ounces of pork and ¼ of a cup of cheese to each tortilla.
4. Tightly roll the tortillas. Line the tortillas onto a greased foil-lined pan.
5. Spray an even coat of cooking oil spray over the tortillas.
6. Air Fry for 7 to 10 minutes or until the tortillas are a golden color, flipping halfway through.

Nutrition: Calories: 334 kcal Protein: 32.03 g Fat: 6.87 g Carbohydrates: 33.92 g

40. Juicy Pork Chops

Preparation Time: 10 minutes

Cooking Time: 16 minutes

Servings: 4

Ingredients:

- 4 pork chops, boneless
- 2 tsp olive oil
- ½ tsp celery seed
- ½ tsp parsley
- ½ tsp granulated onion
- ½ tsp granulated garlic
- ¼ tsp sugar
- ½ tsp salt

Directions:

1. In a small bowl, mix together oil, celery seed, parsley, granulated onion, granulated garlic, sugar, and salt.
2. Rub seasoning mixture all over the pork chops.
3. Place pork chops on the air fryer oven pan and cook at 350 F for 8 minutes
4. Turn pork chops to other side and cook for 8 minutes more.
5. Serve and enjoy.

Nutrition: Calories 279 Fat 22.3 g Carbs 0.6 g Protein 18.1 g

41. Crispy Meatballs

Preparation Time: 10 minutes

Cooking Time: 12 minutes

Servings: 8

Ingredients:

- 1 lb. ground pork
- 1 lb. ground beef
- 1 tbsp. Worcestershire sauce
- ½ cup feta cheese, crumbled
- ½ cup breadcrumbs
- 2 eggs, lightly beaten
- ¼ cup fresh parsley, chopped
- 1 tbsp. garlic, minced
- 1 onion, chopped
- ¼ tsp pepper
- 1 tsp salt

Directions:

1. Add all ingredients into the mixing bowl and mix until well combined.
2. Spray air fryer oven tray pan with cooking spray.

3. Make small balls from meat mixture and arrange on a pan and air fry t 400 F for 10-12 minutes
4. Serve and enjoy.

Nutrition: Calories 263 Fat 9 g Carbs 7.5 g Protein 35.9 g

42. Air fryer Mediterranean Lentil and Collard Soup

Preparation Time: 10 minutes

Cooking Time: 20 minutes

Servings: 6

Ingredients:

- 2 tablespoons of extra virgin olive oil
- 1 medium yellow onion, chopped
- 2 medium celery stocks, diced
- 3 garlic cloves, minced
- 2 teaspoons of ground cumin
- 1 teaspoon of ground turmeric
- 4 cups of low-sodium vegetable broth
- 1 ¼ cup of water
- 1 1/2 cups brown lentils, rinsed in water
- 2 carrots, peeled and diced
- 1 bay leaf
- 1 teaspoon himalayan salt
- ½ teaspoon of ground black pepper
- 3 collard leaves, cut into strips

- 1 teaspoon of lemon juice

Directions:

1. Set air fryer to saute, then add the olive oil, heat, and add onions and celery. Stir often for 5 minutes. Turn the air fryer off.
2. Stir in the garlic, cumin, and turmeric until combined.
3. Add broth, water, lentils, carrots, bay leaf, salt, and pepper. Lock the lid and close the valve. Fix to manual and cook on high pressure for 13 minutes.
4. After completion, quick release the pressure, carefully remove the lid and stir in collards and lemon juice.
5. Make sure to lock the lid and set to manual and cook for 2 more minutes on high. Quick-release the pressure, open the lid, and it's ready to serve.

Nutrition: Calories – 127.9 Protein– 7.3 g Fat – 0.8 g Carbs – 25.9 g.

43. Green Chicken Chili

Preparation Time: 10 minutes

Cooking Time: 35 minutes

Servings: 8

Ingredients:

- 2 tbsp. unsalted butter
- 1 medium yellow onion (to be peeled and chopped)
- ½ lb. poblano peppers (to be seeded and roughly chopped)
- ½ lb. Anaheim peppers (to be seeded and roughly chopped)
- ½ lb. tomatillos (to be husked and quartered)
- 2 small jalapeño peppers (to be seeded and roughly chopped)
- 2 garlic cloves (to be peeled and minced)
- 1 tsp. ground cumin
- 6 bone-in, skin-on chicken thighs (2 ½ lbs. in total)
- 2 cups chicken stock
- 2 cups water
- 1/3 cup roughly chopped fresh cilantro

- 3 cans Great Northern beans (to be drained and rinsed, 15 oz. cans)

Directions:

1. Choose the "Sauté" button on the Air fryer and when hot, add butter to melt. Once the butter melts, add onion and cook for about 3 minutes until softened. Add poblano and Anaheim peppers, then tomatillos, and jalapeños. Cook 3 minutes add garlic and cumin. Cook about 30 seconds or until fragrant. Then cancel sautéing.

2. Add the thighs, stock, and water to pot and stir. Tightly close lid and have the steam release set to the "Sealing" position. Select the "Rice/Grain" option and set the timer for 30 minutes. At the end of the cook time, do a quick release of pressure and open lid to stir well. Press the "Cancel" button and transfer the chicken to a cutting board. After carefully removing the skin, shred the meat with two forks.

3. Using an immersion blender, purée the sauce until smooth. Stir in the meat, cilantro, and beans and serve warm.

Nutrition: Calories – 304 Protein– 33 g Fat – 10 g Carbs – 19 g.

44. Air fryer Italian Beef Stew

Preparation Time: 10 minutes

Cooking Time: 35 minutes

Servings: 6

Ingredients:

- 3 pounds of beef stew
- 1 onion, diced
- 4 carrots, diced
- 8-ounce baby portabella mushrooms, sliced
- 24-ounces of beef broth
- 15 ounce diced tomatoes, canned
- 3 tablespoons of white flour
- 1 teaspoon of dried basil leaves
- 1 teaspoon of dried thyme leaves
- 1 teaspoon of salt
- 1 teaspoon of pepper
- dried parsley

Directions:

1. Place meat in the air fryer.
2. Add in carrots, broth, flour, basil, thyme, salt, pepper, and tomatoes to air fryer and stir.
3. Close the lid.

4. Cook on high pressure for 35 minutes.
5. Quick release the pressure and carefully remove the lid.
6. Stir in the mushroom, stir the soup and then serve.

Nutrition: Calories – 385 Protein– 54 g Fat – 12 g Carbs – 12 g.

45.   Golden Avocado and Tomato Egg Rolls

Preparation Time: 10 minutes

Cooking Time: 5 minutes

Servings: 5

Ingredients:

- 10 egg roll wrappers
- 3 avocados, peeled and pitted
- 1 tomato, diced
- Salt and ground black pepper, to taste
- Cooking spray

Directions:

1. Spritz the air fry basket with cooking spray.
2. Put the avocados and tomato in a food processor. Sprinkle with salt and ground black pepper. Pulse to mix and coarsely mash until smooth.
3. Unfold the wrappers on a clean work surface, then divide the mixture in the center of each wrapper. Roll the wrapper up and press to seal.
4. Transfer the rolls to the basket and spritz with cooking spray.

5. Place the basket on the air fry position.
6. Select Air Fry, set temperature to 350°F (180°C) and set time to 5 minutes. Flip the rolls halfway through the cooking time.
7. When cooked, the rolls should be golden brown.
8. Serve immediately.

Nutrition: Calories 266 Carbs 0.1g Fat 2.8g Protein 4.8g

46. Korean Beef and Onion Tacos

Preparation Time: 1 hour 15 minutes

Cooking Time: 12 minutes

Servings: 6

Ingredients:

- 2 tablespoons gochujang
- 1 tablespoon soy sauce
- 2 tablespoons sesame seeds
- 2 teaspoons minced fresh ginger
- 2 cloves garlic, minced
- 2 tablespoons toasted sesame oil
- 2 teaspoons sugar
- 1/2 teaspoon kosher salt
- 11/2 pounds (680 g) thinly sliced beef chuck
- 1 medium red onion, sliced
- 6 corn tortillas, warmed
- ¼ cup chopped fresh cilantro
- 1/2 cup kimchi
- 1/2 cup chopped green onions

Directions:

1. Combine the ginger, garlic, gochujang, sesame seeds, soy sauce, sesame oil, salt, and sugar in a large bowl. Stir to mix well.
2. Dunk the beef chunk in the large bowl. Press to submerge, then wrap the bowl in plastic and refrigerate to marinate for at least 1 hour.
3. Remove the beef chunk from the marinade and transfer to the air fry basket. Add the onion to the basket.
4. Place the basket on the air fry position.
5. Select Air Fry, set temperature to 400°F (205°C) and set time to 12 minutes. Stir the mixture halfway through the cooking time.
6. When cooked, the beef will be well browned.
7. Unfold the tortillas on a clean work surface, then divide the fried beef and onion on the tortillas. Spread the green onions, kimchi, and cilantro on top.
8. Serve immediately.

Nutrition: Calories 246 Carbs 0.1g Fat 2.8g Protein 10.8g

47. Beefy 'n Cheesy Spanish Rice Casserole

Preparation Time: 10 minutes

Cooking Time: 50 minutes

Servings: 3

Ingredients:

- 2 tablespoons chopped green bell pepper
- 1 tablespoon chopped fresh cilantro
- 1/2-pound lean ground beef
- 1/2 cup water
- 1/2 teaspoon salt
- 1/2 teaspoon brown sugar
- 1/2 pinch ground black pepper
- 1/3 cup uncooked long grain rice
- 1/4 cup finely chopped onion
- 1/4 cup chili sauce
- 1/4 teaspoon ground cumin
- 1/4 teaspoon Worcestershire sauce
- 1/4 cup shredded Cheddar cheese
- 1/2 (14.5 ounce) can canned tomatoes

Directions:

1. Lightly grease baking pan of air fryer with cooking spray. Add ground beef.
2. For 10 minutes, cook on 360°F Halfway through cooking time, stir and crumble beef. Discard excess fat,
3. Stir in pepper, Worcestershire sauce, cumin, brown sugar, salt, chili sauce, rice, water, tomatoes, green bell pepper, and onion. Mix well. Cover pan with foil and cook for 25 minutes. Stirring occasionally
4. Give it one last good stir, press down firmly and sprinkle cheese on top.
5. Cook uncovered for 15 minutes at 390°F until tops are lightly browned.
6. Serve and enjoy with chopped cilantro.

Nutrition: Calories 346 Cal Fat 19.1 g Carbs 0 g Protein 18.5 g

48. Warming Winter Beef with Celery

Preparation Time: 5 minutes

Cooking Time: 12 minutes

Servings: 4

Ingredients:

- 9 ounces tender beef, chopped
- 1/2 cup leeks, chopped
- 1/2 cup celery stalks, chopped
- 2 cloves garlic, smashed
- 2 tablespoons red cooking wine
- 3/4 cup cream of celery soup
- 2 sprigs rosemary, chopped
- 1/4 teaspoon smoked paprika
- 3/4 teaspoons salt
- 1/4 teaspoon black pepper, or to taste

Directions:

1. Add the beef, leeks, celery, and garlic to the baking dish; cook for about 5 minutes at 390 degrees F.
2. Once the meat is starting to tender, pour in the wine and soup. Season with rosemary, smoked paprika, salt, and black pepper
3. Now, cook an additional 7 minutes

Nutrition: Calories 364 Cal Fat 9 g Carbs 39 g Protein 32 g

49. Beef & veggie Spring Rolls

Preparation Time: 5 minutes

Cooking Time: 12 minutes

Servings: 10

Ingredients:

- 2-ounce Asian rice noodles
- 1 tablespoon sesame oil
- 7-ounce ground beef
- 1 small onion, chopped
- 3 garlic cloves, crushed
- 1 cup fresh mixed vegetables
- 1 teaspoon soy sauce
- 1 packet spring roll skins
- 2 tablespoons water
- Olive oil, as required

Directions:

1. Soak the noodles in warm water till soft.
2. Dry out and cut into small lengths. In a pan heat the oil and add the onion and garlic and sauté for about 4-5 minutes
3. Add beef and cook for about 4-5 minutes
4. Add vegetables and cook for about 5-7 minutes or till cooked through.

5. Stir in soy sauce and remove from the heat.
6. Immediately, stir in the noodles and keep aside till all the juices have been absorbed.
7. Preheat the Air Fryer Oven to 350 degrees F.
8. Place the spring rolls skin onto a smooth surface.
9. Add a line of the filling diagonally across.
10. Fold the top point over the filling and then fold in both sides.
11. On the final point, brush it with water before rolling to seal.
12. Brush the spring rolls with oil.
13. Arrange the rolls in batches in the air fryer and Cook for about 8 minutes
14. Repeat with remaining rolls. Now, place spring rolls onto a baking sheet.
15. Bake it for about 6 minutes per side.

Nutrition: Calories 364 Cal Fat 9 g Carbs 39 g Protein 32 g

50. Charred Onions and Steak Cube BBQ

Preparation Time: 5 minutes

Cooking Time: 40 minutes

Servings: 3

Ingredients:

- 1 cup red onions cut into wedges
- 1 tablespoon dry mustard
- 1 tablespoon olive oil
- 1-pound boneless beef sirloin, cut into cubes
- Salt and pepper to taste

Directions:

1. Preheat the air fryer to 390°F.
2. Place the grill pan accessory in the air fryer.
3. Toss all ingredients in a bowl and mix until everything is coated with the seasonings.
4. Place on the grill pan and cook for 40 minutes
5. Halfway through the cooking time, give a stir to cook evenly.

Nutrition: Calories 260 Cal Fat 10.7 g Carbs 0 g Protein 35.5 g

CONCLUSION

Thank you for the support on this book.

Air Fryer Grill is a new air fryer that is designed to be able to cook multiple foods at once, whether they are grilled, steamed or fried at different temperatures simultaneously without slowing down cooking time between foods.

Here are some tips to best use this appliance,

1. Do not use metal utensils.

You should not use metal utensils such as forks, spoons, or knives to stir food while

cooking with the Air Fryer Grill. Metal utensils can scratch and damage the nonstick coating inside the cooking basket.

2. Foods cooked on a grill may dry out easily and quickly.

Foods cooked on a grill may dry out quickly because of the high heat and lack of fat or liquids in foods like chicken breast or steaks. Add oil to meats right before you put them on the grill to keep them moist and juicy, but be sure not to overdo it as this will change taste preference.

3. Use a silicone or rubber spatula to move cooked foods around in the basket for even cooking.

Silicone, nylon, and rubber spatulas are designed to be used on nonstick surfaces and will not scratch the cooking surface of your Air Fryer Grill.

4. Most food cooked on a grill is somewhat dry after cooking.

If you prefer things crunchy, try seasoning meat or vegetables with salt and pepper right before putting it on the grill for higher heat expediency and faster cooking time.

5. You can use the Air Fryer Grill to cook frozen food as long as you leave some space between each piece of frozen food so that it cooks evenly.

6. There is a maximum load of 1500g of food in the Air Fryer Grill.

7. Use the temperature probe to check the internal temperature of fish or meat and the food will be done in time.

8. It cannot only cook, but also is used as a slow cooker, griddle, steamer and maker, No need to waste time on cooking for several days!

9. Do not use really cold water when cleaning; it will make the coating discolored or damaged; do not clean with chemicals directly either.

10. We have designed the Air Fryer to make any kind of food taste delicious, so please try to use seasoning of your choice.

11. If you leave the Air Fryer for a long time with the power on, the temperature will rise. Turn off the power first and then unplug it so that it does not overheat.

12. Do not preheat before adding food.

Preheating the Air Fryer at a low temperature for a short time will cause food to dry and lose flavor.

13. Do not use the basket to store other types of utensils.

The nonstick coating on the bottom part of the Air Basket may get damaged easily.

14. If the temperature drops unexpectedly, place the power cover over your Air Fryer Grill to prevent heat loss, also be sure to press in the air vent in order to release pressure inside cooking basket (This is especially important when cooking chicken breasts or steaks.)

Again, thank you for your support on this book.

CPSIA information can be obtained
at www.ICGtesting.com
Printed in the USA
BVHW090011080621
608941BV00004B/1073

9 781802 861075